The Tides of Transformation

Waves rise high and then retreat,
Carrying dreams on their soft beat.
Each swell whispers stories untold,
Transformations in depths unfold.

Seas change colors in the night,
Reflecting whispers of the light.
Old forms dissolve in the embrace,
Emerging anew, finding their place.

The Light Breaking Through

Darkness fades as dawn appears,
Soft light dances, calming fears.
Golden rays touch every tree,
Illuminating paths to be.

Shadows retreat into the past,
The promise of day comes at last.
Hope emerges in warm embrace,
Guiding hearts to a brighter space.

New Horizons Await

Beyond the hills, the skies expand,
New journeys call, a guiding hand.
Every step leads to the unknown,
With courage, seeds of dreams are sown.

Mountains echo with voices clear,
Whispers of hope, drawing near.
As the dawn ignites the day,
New horizons light the way.

A Dawn Untold

In the silence, dreams arise,
Veiled in mystery, they mesmerize.
A dawn untold, a canvas bright,
Awaits the brush of morning light.

Colors swirl and gently blend,
Each hue a tale, a promise penned.
With every heartbeat, life unfolds,
In the dawn's embrace, the future holds.

Unwritten Pages

In the quiet of night, thoughts arise,
Ink flows softly, beneath starlit skies.
Every whisper, a story untold,
Dreams weave magic, in pages of gold.

Blank spaces gleam, like treasures unchained,
Each heartbeat a verse, joy and pain.
Future chapters wait, with hope at the door,
The tale of a life, forever in store.

A Canvas of Tomorrow

Colors blending, brush in hand,
Vision painted across the land.
Every stroke, a choice we make,
In this canvas, futures awake.

Shadows linger, yet light will shine,
Every hue, a path divine.
With dreams as our guide, we explore the unknown,
Creating a world that's ours alone.

Shattered Chains

Bound no more, we rise and stand,
Writing history, hand in hand.
Chains of doubt crumble away,
Tomorrow shimmers, bright as day.

Voices echo, strong and clear,
In unity, we persevere.
Strength in numbers, courage in heart,
Together anew, we make a fresh start.

The Blooming After Winter

Fragrant whispers in the breeze,
Petals unfurling with such ease.
Winter's chill now fades away,
Nature dances, bright and gay.

Sunlight kisses the frozen ground,
Life emerges, all around.
In every bud, a promise awake,
The world reborn, for spring's sweet sake.

From Old to Bold

Once upon a weary day,
Dreams lay dormant, out of sight.
But whispers stirred within the air,
Inviting sparks to take their flight.

Shadows grew from fading light,
Yet courage found a voice to sing.
With each step, the heart took flight,
Embracing change in blossoming spring.

The past, a guide, but not the chain,
Each lesson learned, a coloring hue.
From every loss, a stronger gain,
The boldness formed from what we knew.

The Alchemy of Change

In the crucible of night,
Dreams are melded, hopes conjoined.
With every tear, a new delight,
From ashes rise, old paths refined.

Time flows like liquid gold,
Carving rivers, strong and free.
Embrace the shift, be brave, be bold,
For change unveils our destiny.

What was solid turns to air,
And every fear begins to fade.
In transformation's tender care,
We find the strength to be remade.

New Footprints in Time

In the sands where stories tread,
New footprints mark the path ahead.
With every step, adventures bloom,
Echoing the heart's sweet tune.

Each moment holds a seed of grace,
Nurtured by the dreams we chase.
The future calls, a siren's song,
With whispered promises so strong.

We carve our names in light and shade,
Where memories and hopes cascade.
Through every turn, we boldly stride,
Into the dawn, with hearts open wide.

A Garden of Possibilities

In the soil of our delight,
Seeds of wonder, bold and bright.
Watered with love and trust so deep,
A garden grows where dreams can leap.

Each flower tells a tale anew,
Of journeys past, of skies so blue.
Roots intertwine, forming a bond,
In this haven, we grow fond.

With every petal, hope takes flight,
Embracing risks, chasing the light.
A tapestry of thoughts entwined,
In this space, our souls unwind.

Rivers of Change

A gentle flow through valleys deep,
Whispers secrets that rivers keep.
With every turn, a story told,
In currents warm and waters cold.

Mountains watch as banks erode,
Nature's path, a winding road.
The future glimmers, bright and clear,
In every bend, a hope sincere.

Leaves dance lightly in the breeze,
While time flows softly, seeking ease.
Embrace the tide that sweeps you hence,
For in the current lies the sense.

As seasons shift and shadows fall,
Rivers of change will heed the call.
In flowing grace, we find our way,
Towards a dawn of a brand new day.

Breaking Old Shells

A fragile shell that once confined,
Holds within a heart refined.
With each crack, the light breaks through,
A promise bright, a life anew.

The world outside, vast and wide,
Calls to those who wish to glide.
Beneath the surface, shadows blend,
But courage brings the light to mend.

With every tremor, a new birth's song,
The spirit soars, where it belongs.
Let go the fears that held you tight,
Embrace the dawn, step into light.

For growth awaits, in vibrant hues,
A butterfly that will not lose.
In breaking shells, we shall unveil,
The beauty found beyond the pale.

Eclipsed by the Sun

A shadow falls, the day grows dim,
As twilight blurs the edges grim.
But in the dark, the stars ignite,
In whispers shared, they weave the light.

The moon ascends, with gentle grace,
Enfolding night in soft embrace.
Yet every shadow sings a tune,
A dance between the sun and moon.

As moments pass, the light returns,
The flickering flame of hope still burns.
In eclipsed paths, we find our way,
Through darkness brightens the day.

So cherish both the light and shade,
For in their blend, true beauty's made.
With every cycle, life will show,
The balance found in ebb and flow.

The First Step Forward

A timid heart begins to race,
As dreams unfold in open space.
Each moment whispers, take a chance,
Embrace the fear and join the dance.

The road ahead may twist and turn,
But every step, new lessons learned.
With every breath, a leap of faith,
A journey born in life's embrace.

Let not the doubts weigh heavy still,
For courage stirs beneath the will.
In tiny strides, the path unfolds,
As stories of the brave retold.

With open arms, the future calls,
In every rise, in every fall.
So take your step, let life explore,
For every end is just the door.

Horizons Untouched

Beyond the mountains, skies align,
Wonders call from lands unknown.
Each step forward, a silent sign,
In dreams, the seeds of courage sown.

Echoes dance on winds so free,
Paths of light unfurl ahead.
With every glance, the heart can see,
New worlds await where fears have fled.

The Whisper of Change

In gentle breezes, futures stir,
The past will fade but lessons stay.
With every nod, the heart will purr,
Embracing life in a brand new way.

Softly, time unveils its song,
A melody of hopes reborn.
With every note, we join the throng,
Renewed by dawn, our spirits worn.

Where Hope Takes Root

In quiet corners, dreams will grow,
Tenders sprouts from earth so deep.
With love and care, the heart will know,
Hope's gentle promise, ours to keep.

Through storms and trials, strive we must,
Resilience blooms where shadows dwell.
In every struggle, place your trust,
For hope is magic, cast its spell.

A Symphony of Fresh Chapters

Each page turns, a story unfolds,
With whispers of journeys yet to start.
In every word, the adventure holds,
The rhythm and pulse of the beating heart.

As colors blend in twilight's cue,
The canvas stretches, wide and vast.
A symphony born from visions true,
Creating tales that forever last.

A Heart Willing to Wander

In meadows wide, my heart takes flight,
Through whispered winds, beneath the light.
It dances free, with dreams to chase,
In every corner, it finds its place.

A restless spirit, seeking the sea,
Each wave that crashes, beckons me.
With every journey, I seek to find,
The pieces that make this heart unwind.

Mountains towering, calling my name,
Their rugged edges ignite a flame.
Through valleys deep, my soul explores,
In every step, a new world soars.

With stars above as my guiding light,
I forge ahead through the endless night.
A heart that wanders, yet feels at home,
In every journey, forever to roam.

Blossoming into Now

In gardens rich, where colors bloom,
I find my peace, dispelling gloom.
Each petal soft, a story told,
Of dreams and hopes, of hearts turned bold.

The sun's warm rays, a gentle kiss,
Awaken life, it's purest bliss.
With every sunrise, I dare to grow,
Embracing moments, the ebb and flow.

In fragrant whispers, I hear the call,
To shed the past and rise from fall.
With roots so deep, I stand my ground,
In every heartbeat, my joy is found.

With each new dawn, my spirit thrives,
In every moment, true love strives.
I blossom wide, a vibrant show,
In all of life, I'm learning to glow.

A Fresh Canvas Awaits

The dawn breaks soft and bright,
A palette rich in hues,
Each stroke a dream in flight,
A world that's ours to choose.

With every brush we make,
A story starts to blend,
Emotions that we wake,
A journey with no end.

The whispers of the muse,
Inspire each gentle line,
In shades we brightly choose,
New echoes intertwine.

Let go of shades of gray,
Embrace the vibrant now,
For on this fresh display,
We'll find the truest vow.

Horizons Yet to See

Beyond the hills we climb,
The sun begins to rise,
With every step in time,
New vistas greet our eyes.

The path is wide and free,
With wonders yet to find,
We chase the glinting sea,
And leave the past behind.

In dreams of light we soar,
Through clouds of hopes anew,
Each moment we explore,
Reveals a broader view.

The heartbeats of the earth,
Guide footprints on the sand,
For in this place of birth,
We make a life so grand.

The Dance of New Life

Awake, the world does sing,
In colors bold and bright,
Each bloom a whispered thing,
In morning's tender light.

The leaves begin to sway,
A rhythm soft and sweet,
As nature finds its way,
In life's resounding beat.

With every breath we take,
New stories start to flow,
From every leap we make,
The warmth begins to grow.

Join in this vibrant dance,
Embrace the chance to thrive,
In every spin, a glance,
We celebrate our drive.

Shadows Fleeing

As twilight whispers low,
The stars begin to gleam,
In shadows, hopes will grow,
Embracing every dream.

The night unveils its lace,
A curtain drawn with care,
Each moment finds its grace,
In silvered moonlit air.

We chase the fleeting dusk,
With courage in our hearts,
In whispers soft, we trust,
That light forever starts.

So let the shadows go,
And rise with every dawn,
For in the light we know,
A new day's never gone.

Beyond Yesterday's Shadows

In whispers soft, the night is still,
Memories linger, time to fill.
A journey starts where dreams collide,
Beyond the fears we often hide.

Colors fade, and silence reigns,
Yet hope within the heart still gains.
With every step, the past unwinds,
Leaving shadows, truth it finds.

Fleeting moments dance on air,
Embracing all, both light and care.
Underneath the starry veil,
A new beginning makes us pale.

So let us rise with courage bold,
From yesterday, our souls unfold.
With open hearts, we chase the gleam,
Beyond the shadows, life's bright dream.

Journey into the Unknown

With every breath, the path awaits,
A world of wonder radiates.
Through valleys deep and mountains high,
Curiosity will fly.

Each step we take, a mystery,
Unlocking doors of history.
The stars above will guide our way,
As night embraces breaking day.

Yet fears may rise, like morning mist,
With every doubt, we still persist.
The thrill of life compels our hearts,
In every ending, new world starts.

So let us venture, hand in hand,
To lands unseen, we'll make our stand.
With dreams to chase, and stories spun,
Our journey starts, the tale begun.

Steps into the Clear

The morning light begins to break,
As shadows fade with every shake.
Each step we take, the world anew,
With visions bright, and skies of blue.

Through fields of gold, we weave and roam,
Finding comfort, feels like home.
With every stride, our hearts take flight,
Embracing warmth of purest light.

Let go of doubts, release the pain,
In open air, there's much to gain.
Together, we will face the vast,
Step into clear, leave pain of past.

So walk with me on this bright shore,
With every moment, we'll explore.
The beauty lies in paths we find,
Steps into clear, our souls aligned.

Reflections of a New Dawn

The sun ascends, a golden grace,
Awakening dreams, time to embrace.
In every shadow, lessons learned,
With open hearts, the fire burned.

Through mirrored skies, we see the truth,
The joy of life, the song of youth.
Each dawn a canvas, fresh and bright,
Painted softly with hope and light.

As night gives way to morning's call,
We rise again, no fear to fall.
With every breath, the past subsides,
Reflections new, like rising tides.

In every heart, a spark ignites,
A promise made in soaring heights.
Together we will find our way,
Reflections found in each new day.

Flames of Transformation

In shadows deep, a spark ignites,
The old must fade, embrace new heights.
From ashes rise, the spirit gleams,
A dance of hope, a blaze of dreams.

With every flicker, doubt departs,
A molten heart, reformed in parts.
Through trials fierce, we find our way,
In fire's glow, we dare to stay.

The journey calls, to forge anew,
In passion's grip, our courage grew.
The flames will shape what we will be,
A phoenix born, wild and free.

With every burn, a lesson learned,
The path of change, through fire turned.
We move ahead, with hearts aglow,
In flames of transformation, we flow.

Reimagining the Path

Beneath the stars, a trail unfolds,
New dreams arise, as courage molds.
With every step, the ground we trace,
A daring quest, we embrace.

In whispered winds, ideas bloom,
A world reborn, dispelling gloom.
Paths intertwine, like branches wide,
In unity, we take our stride.

Each choice we make, a stone we lay,
A vibrant path, in bright array.
With open hearts, we draw the map,
In reimagining, we bridge the gap.

The journey calls, with each refrain,
To seek the light, to dance in rain.
With visions bold, we chart the way,
In reimagining the path, we sway.

Tides of Rebirth

The ocean whispers to the shore,
A tale of change, forevermore.
With every wave, a cycle spins,
In tides of rebirth, life begins.

The moon commands the waters deep,
A promise made, a secret keep.
As currents shift, old forms decay,
New life emerges, come what may.

In flowing rhythms, hearts align,
The past releases, we redefine.
With courage swells, we meet the day,
As tides of rebirth guide our way.

With every crest, a chance to rise,
To face the storm, to touch the skies.
In unity with nature's art,
We find the strength to play our part.

Threads of New Fabric

A loom of life, where colors blend,
In every stitch, a heartfelt mend.
The fibers weave, with stories told,
In threads of new fabric, we unfold.

Each pattern formed, unique and bright,
In every twist, we find our light.
The tapestry of dreams we share,
Embodies love, and shows we care.

With hands entwined, we craft the scene,
Of joys and trials, space in between.
Together strong, we face the fray,
In threads of new fabric, we stay.

So let us weave, with hearts sincere,
Turn frayed edges into cheer.
For in this cloth, our spirits blend,
In threads of new fabric, there's no end.

Unfolding Petals

In the quiet of dawn's light,
Colors start to bloom bright.
Whispers float through the air,
Nature wakes from her lair.

Each petal, a soft embrace,
Reveals beauty with grace.
Gentle raindrops fall down,
Kissing earth with a crown.

Morning sun starts to rise,
Painting gold in the skies.
Life begins to ignite,
As darkness takes flight.

With each breath, hope anew,
The world wears a bright hue.
Unfolding in splendid time,
Nature's rhythm, a rhyme.

The Promise of Another Day

When shadows fade to grey,
A new dawn finds its way.
Hope lingers in the air,
Whispers of dreams laid bare.

The sun climbs up with might,
Chasing away the night.
Every ray tells a tale,
Of courage that won't fail.

With open hearts we tread,
On paths we've never led.
Holding tight to our dreams,
Life is more than it seems.

Each moment feels so bright,
Guided by softer light.
Together we will stay,
Embracing a new day.

Seeds Beneath Snow

In the stillness of the night,
Lie the seeds, out of sight.
Blanketed soft and white,
Awaiting spring's delight.

Silent whispers in the cold,
Stories waiting to unfold.
Under snow, dreams persist,
Yearning for the sun's kiss.

Time, a gentle caress,
Nature's quiet success.
With patience, life will grow,
From the dark, seeds bestow.

Soon the thaw will draw near,
Life will rise, free from fear.
What was once hidden deep,
Awakens from its sleep.

A Second Wind

When the world feels heavy,
And the path seems unsteady,
A breath ignites the flame,
Reviving hope once again.

The heart beats strong and bold,
With stories yet untold.
Each step a dance of fate,
Embracing life, not late.

Winds may change their course,
But we find our own source.
With every gentle push,
Strength returns in a rush.

So rise with this new dawn,
The past forever gone.
Feel the light as it sings,
A gift that life now brings.

New Beginnings

In the quiet dawn's embrace,
A chance to start anew,
Hope dances in the air,
With each day breaking through.

Pathways once overgrown,
Now bloom with vibrant light,
Every step, a seed is sown,
In the warmth of the night.

Dreams that seemed out of reach,
Now take shape, collide,
The world becomes a canvas,
As fate becomes our guide.

With courage, fears dissolve,
The heart begins to sing,
Embracing what's to come,
In life's unending spring.

Dawn's Whisper

The sky blushes soft and clear,
Whispers of light unfold,
An orchestra of dreams near,
As daybreak's tale is told.

Gentle breezes start to play,
Caressing leaves and grass,
Painting shadows in the fray,
As night begins to pass.

Each moment feels like gold,
Promises linger long,
In the warmth we can hold,
Life's sweet, tender song.

With eyes closed, hearts will soar,
To a rhythm divine,
In the hush, we explore,
Dawn's secrets intertwine.

The First Breath of Spring

Blossoms break through winter's white,
Colors burst, alive and bright,
Gentle rains kiss thirsty ground,
A symphony of life is found.

Birds return with songs of cheer,
Echoing the warmth that's near,
Sunlight dances on the stream,
Awakening each dormant dream.

The world awakes, a vibrant scene,
Green shoots reach where snow has been,
A canvas fresh, anew we sing,
With joy, we greet the spring.

In every bud, a promise lies,
Of love that blooms beneath the skies,
Nature's dance, a sweet embrace,
In springtime's glow, life finds its place.

Rebirth in the Morning Light

The sun peeks over hills anew,
Casting shadows, fresh and true,
Each ray a whisper, soft and bright,
Waking dreams in morning light.

From the depths of darkest night,
Emerges hope, a glorious sight,
Life finds its way to rise and soar,
As the heart begins to explore.

Past sorrows fade with golden dawn,
New paths are paved, the old are gone,
In every breath, a spark ignites,
Rebirth dances in the heights.

With every step, the soul aligns,
In the glow, our heart defines,
Transformed by warmth, we feel the thrill,
In morning's light, our dreams fulfill.

Painting with New Colors

Brush in hand, I start to see,
A world of hues, so wild and free.
Each stroke reveals a secret tone,
In shades of joy, I'm not alone.

Canvas whispers soft and clear,
The stories told, drawing near.
With every blend, a vision grows,
In vibrant dreams, my spirit flows.

Colors dance beneath my gaze,
Transforming thoughts into a blaze.
From grey to gold, a life anew,
My heart reborn in vivid view.

So here I stand, a painter bold,
Creating magic yet untold.
With new colors, I paint my fate,
A masterpiece that won't wait.

Uncharted Waters Ahead

The horizon calls with whispers soft,
A journey waits, where dreams take off.
Uncharted paths invite the brave,
To sail beyond the open wave.

With winds of change that fill the sail,
Adventure waits, I cannot fail.
Each wave that crashes, wild and new,
Leads me forth to skies of blue.

The map's unwritten, but feel the spark,
As I embrace the vast and dark.
With courage firm, I chart my course,
Into the depths, a mighty force.

Here in the sea, I'm bound to find,
The strength of heart, the open mind.
With every stroke, I'll carve my way,
To shores of gold, come what may.

Becoming Unbound

With shackles broke, I stretch my wings,
A world awaits, so vast, it sings.
No longer held by fears of old,
In freedom's light, my dreams unfold.

Through open skies, I soar and dive,
Each moment lived, I feel alive.
The weight of doubt, I cast away,
Embracing now, my brand new day.

Beyond the walls that held me tight,
I find my strength, I seek the light.
With every step, a path appears,
In joy and laughter, I shed my tears.

A spirit wild, no chains can bind,
In this journey, I seek to find.
Who I am, and who I'll be,
Becoming unbound, wild and free.

Sunrise Over the Old World

A gentle glow breaks through the night,
With colors bold and pure delight.
The dawn arrives, a quiet grace,
Awakens dreams in every place.

The shadows fade, the day begins,
With hope reborn as daylight wins.
The old world stirs, refreshed and bright,
A canvas new, in morning light.

Each ray of sun, a promise made,
With every heartbeat, fears allayed.
In every corner, life will bloom,
Embracing light, dispelling gloom.

Oh, how the earth begins to sing,
As nature wakes, unfurling spring.
With sunrise bright, the old is new,
A world transformed, in every hue.

Whispers of Tomorrow

In the quiet hour, shadows glide,
Dreams weave tales where hopes reside.
Echoes hum of what's to come,
Softly calling, the future's drum.

Stars will dance in velvet skies,
Guiding hearts with whispered sighs.
New dawn breaks, a canvas bare,
Carving paths through tranquil air.

Hope ignites with morning light,
Casting away the cloak of night.
Every moment, a gem to hold,
Whispers weave the brave and bold.

In stillness, we find our way,
To embrace the coming day.
With whispers soft, the world ignites,
As tomorrow blooms in vibrant sights.

The Blank Canvas

A canvas wide, untouched, untamed,
A world of colors yet unnamed.
Each brush a thought, each stroke a dream,
A life uncharted, a boundless theme.

Whispers of shades, of dark and light,
Inspire creation, ignite the night.
With every hue, a story told,
In swirls of passion, brave and bold.

A palette waits, with promise bright,
To capture visions in the night.
Every line a journey starts,
In vibrant strokes, the soul imparts.

Here lies potential, wild and free,
To paint the life we long to see.
With each attempt, we find our voice,
In art we trust, we make our choice.

Awakening Potential

Deep within, a spark ignites,
A fire stirs in quiet nights.
Dreams awaken, eyes unclose,
In this moment, life bestows.

Through the valley, whispers call,
Unseen forces, we will sprawl.
Each heartbeat echoes with intent,
Unlocking strength, pure and unspent.

Paths unfurl with every breath,
Breaking barriers, defying death.
Wings unfold, reaching for the sky,
In potential's dance, we learn to fly.

The journey starts with trust in self,
Unveiling wealth in inner health.
Awaken now, your heart's own song,
With each step forward, you belong.

Voyage to Possibilities

On waves of dreams, we set our sail,
To chase horizons beyond the pale.
Each gust of wind, a call to roam,
In every heartbeat, we find home.

Islands of hope break through the mist,
With treasures waiting, we can't resist.
The compass of faith guides our way,
To realms where colors brightly play.

In every tide, a chance observed,
To seek the paths that we deserve.
Cast off the doubts, embrace the sea,
In this voyage, we learn to be.

Together we navigate the unknown,
In unity, strength beautifully shown.
For in our hearts, the map unfolds,
A journey of love, a tale of bold.

The Adventure of Renewal

In the heart of the forest, shadows play,
A journey begins on a brand-new day.
With whispers of hope in every breeze,
Nature hums softly, putting us at ease.

Streams sparkle bright as they twist and turn,
Each step forward, a lesson to learn.
The path unfolds with secrets untold,
A tapestry woven in colors bold.

Mountains stand tall, reaching for the skies,
In lofty peaks, our spirits arise.
We dance with the winds, as laughter surrounds,
In the symphony of life, joy abounds.

With every breath, we release the old,
Embracing the warmth, the new stories unfold.
In the adventure of renewal, we find our way,
Transforming our fears, come what may.

Beyond the Old Fences

There's a world that waits outside the gate,
Where dreams are nurtured, not left to fate.
With every step, curiosity stirs,
Beyond the old fences, adventure purrs.

Fields of golden flowers stretch far and wide,
In the sunlight's glow, we feel alive.
Each moment a treasure, fragile yet bright,
Exploring the wonders that dance in the light.

With laughter shared and stories exchanged,
We break the barriers that once felt strange.
In the bond of friendship, horizons expand,
Together we're stronger, hand in hand.

So let's climb the hills, where the air is clear,
Past the old fences, there's nothing to fear.
In the heart of the unknown, we find our grace,
Beyond the old fences, a magical place.

The Phoenix's Song

From ashes we rise, with wings spread wide,
The spirit ignites in a fierce, colorful tide.
With flames that dance, we reclaim our place,
In the symphony of life, we find our space.

The trials we faced, like sand through time,
Have shaped our path with endurance sublime.
In every heartbeat, a story unfolds,
A melody born from the brave and the bold.

Beneath the dark skies, we seek the light,
Embracing our power, igniting the night.
A phoenix shall soar, reborn from the flame,
In the tapestry of life, we'll never be the same.

So let the world witness our vibrant rise,
As we sing our song, painting endless skies.
In the hearts of the dreamers, we find our song,
The phoenix's call, eternally strong.

Awakening the Dreamer Within

In the still of the night, the stars shine bright,
Whispers of dreams begin to ignite.
Awaking the spirit, so eager to soar,
Unlocking the magic, revealing the door.

Close your eyes gently, breathe in the chance,
Let the heart guide you into a dance.
With visions unfolding like petals anew,
The dreamer awakens, embracing the view.

Through valleys of wonder and mountains of hope,
We gather our courage to learn how to cope.
In the canvas of life, we paint our own hue,
Awakening dreams that are vibrant and true.

So listen closely, hear the call deep,
For the dreamer within, no longer must sleep.
With each step we take, a new world begins,
Awakening the dreamer, where magic spins.

Colors of a New Day

A canvas spreads across the skies,
With hues of gold that gently rise.
Soft whispers of dawn brush the land,
Awakening dreams, so close at hand.

The azure dances, bright and clear,
While crimson tears away the fear.
Emerald fields in morning light,
Invite our hearts to take to flight.

Pastels swirl in a joyful play,
As night recedes, making way.
Each shade a promise, fresh and bold,
A story of wonders yet untold.

Embrace the warmth, let go the chill,
In colors of hope, our spirits fill.
With every dawn, a chance to grow,
In the vibrant hues of a new glow.

From Ashes We Rise

Amidst the charred remains we stand,
With whispers of hope in a trembling hand.
From darkest nights, a fire ignites,
Resilience blooms in the shattered sights.

The embers of dreams refuse to die,
In the silence, we hear our sigh.
From ashes cold, we seek the flame,
In every heart, a spark of the same.

Together we gather, strong and proud,
Voices united, we sing aloud.
Through trials faced and burdens shared,
With every step, we show we cared.

What once was lost can be reborn,
Through storms of life, we'll not be worn.
With courage rising, we take our place,
From ashes we soar, in love's embrace.

Wings of a New Beginning

Beneath the sky, our dreams take flight,
With wings unfurled, we greet the light.
Each heartbeat echoes, bold and true,
In the wide expanse, we'll find the new.

The winds of change whisper sweetly now,
Guiding the way, teaching us how.
To leave behind the chains of the past,
And soar through clouds, horizons vast.

On currents of hope, we dance above,
Fueled by the warmth of endless love.
In unity, we break the mold,
With visions bright and hearts of gold.

Together we rise, no fear in sight,
With every breath, we claim our right.
To embrace the dawn of what's to come,
With wings of faith, we will overcome.

A Journey Reimagined

Step by step, a new path unfolds,
With tales of wonder, yet to be told.
We leave behind what we once knew,
In the spirit of adventure, we renew.

The road is winding, full of surprise,
With every turn, a chance to rise.
Each moment cherished, held so dear,
In laughter and dreams, we conquer fear.

With open hearts, we chase the sun,
In the dance of life, we find our fun.
Through valleys low and mountains high,
We weave our stories beneath the sky.

So let us wander, hand in hand,
In this journey, we'll make our stand.
For every step connects our souls,
In this reimagined life, we are whole.

Blossoms of Change

In springtime's gentle breeze we find,
New blooms awaken, colors unwind.
Each petal whispers tales untold,
Of hopes renewed and dreams of old.

Change is a dance, a rhythmic sway,
As seasons shift from night to day.
With every step, we learn to grow,
Embracing paths we may not know.

The blossoms nod with morning's light,
A promise held beyond our sight.
In fragile forms, strength can arise,
Transforming fears into the skies.

With every bloom, a chance to see,
The beauty in life's mystery.
Together we stand, hand in hand,
In the garden of change, we make our stand.

The Reset Button

When chaos reigns and shadows loom,
A quiet pause dispels the gloom.
In stillness found, we breathe anew,
To glimpse the world from a fresh view.

Hit reset on the daily grind,
Release the weight, unchain the mind.
With every breath, release the pain,
Let hope be more than just a gain.

The power lies within the choice,
To find our path and lift our voice.
A second chance, a brand new start,
Reconnect with the beating heart.

So take a moment, press that key,
Embrace the change, let your soul be free.
In the silence, the truth will shine,
The reset button brings peace divine.

Echoes of Yesterday's Lessons

In the corridors of time we tread,
With echoes of things once said.
The past holds keys, both wise and true,
Guiding our steps in all we do.

Memories linger, shadows play,
Charting the course of our today.
Each lesson learned, a guiding light,
Illuminates the dark of night.

Whispers of caution, calls to be bold,
In every story, treasures hold.
The tapestry we weave takes shape,
From threads of love, and heartache's scrape.

Embrace the past, don't let it bind,
For wisdom flows in hearts refined.
With every echo, we find our way,
Leading us gently to the day.

Dreams in a New Light

When night falls soft and stars ignite,
The dreams we weave take to their flight.
In whispered hopes and visions clear,
We chase the dawn that draws us near.

With every dawn, a canvas waits,
To paint the dreams that hope creates.
Colors blend, horizons wide,
With heart and soul, we take the ride.

No dream too large, no wish too small,
In the embrace of life's sweet call.
For dreams, they bloom in morning's grace,
Reflecting light in every place.

So grasp the moment, hold it tight,
As dreams awaken in the light.
With open hearts, let's soar and fly,
In dreams reborn, we touch the sky.

Sailing Into New Seas

With sails unfurled, we chase the breeze,
Across the waves, where hearts find ease.
The sun dips low, a golden hue,
New horizons call, adventures due.

The stars above, our map tonight,
In whispered winds, our dreams take flight.
We leave the shore, the past behind,
In every wave, new paths we find.

Together we chart, uncharted lands,
Through storms and calm, with steady hands.
The ocean deep, our spirits free,
Sailing forth into the sea.

In twilight's glow, we dance and weave,
In every moment, we believe.
For on this journey, vast and wide,
New seas await, with hope as guide.

The Symphony of New Beginnings

A note is struck, the silence breaks,
In morning's light, the heart awakes.
With every chord, a story springs,
The dawn unfolds, as the chorus sings.

Each moment breathes a tune of grace,
Embracing change in time and space.
The canvas bright, with colors bold,
New dreams arise, waiting to be told.

Together we weave a melody,
In every note, life's harmony.
With open hearts, we let it flow,
The symphony of what's to grow.

And as we play, our spirits soar,
In every heartbeat, we explore.
Through music's depths, we find the voice,
Of new beginnings, in joyous choice.

Echoes into Tomorrow

Whispers drift on winds of time,
Carried forth in rhythm and rhyme.
Memories linger, soft and clear,
As echoes call, we draw them near.

The future beckons, a bright allure,
With each new step, our dreams secure.
Through shadows cast and light that gleams,
We chase the pulse of hopeful dreams.

In the silence, we hear the song,
Of paths once tread, where we belong.
In every heartbeat, a promise made,
Of life unfolding, unafraid.

So let the echoes guide our way,
Into tomorrow, come what may.
For in the journey, we shall find,
The beauty of our hearts aligned.

The Adventure of Unknowing

With every step, the road unfolds,
In every twist, a story holds.
We walk the path, though shadows cling,
Embracing all that life may bring.

In uncertainty, we find our spark,
Through hidden trails, igniting dark.
Each stumble shapes our daring quest,
In unknowing, we find our best.

The thrill of risk, the joy of flight,
In leaps of faith, we chase the light.
With open hearts and spirits free,
The adventure calls, come dance with me.

So let us wander, let us roam,
In uncharted lands, we will find home.
For in this journey, wild and true,
The adventure lies in me and you.

The Art of Letting Go

With tender hands, we release the past,
Memories fade, like shadows cast.
Each moment cherished, never lost,
In freedom's breath, we find our cost.

Lessons learned, like whispers fall,
Strength emerges from every stall.
In the silence, we find our way,
Embracing dawn, we greet the day.

The weight we carried, now a breeze,
Time's gentle touch brings us to ease.
Letting go is a dance of grace,
In open hearts, we find our place.

So here we stand, our spirits high,
With open wings, we learn to fly.
The art of letting go is sweet,
In newfound hope, our souls complete.

In the Heart of Renewal

Beneath the frost, the earth breathes slow,
A tender whisper, a soft glow.
Life unfolds in colors bright,
Awakening dreams, dispelling night.

Petals bloom with morning's kiss,
Every moment, a chance for bliss.
In the heart of renewal, we stand,
With open arms, we make our plans.

Rivers flow with stories old,
Through valleys green, our hopes unfold.
Nature sings a timeless song,
In the heart of change, we belong.

Gathered strength from roots set deep,
In the soil of peace, our spirits leap.
Embracing growth, we face the sun,
In the heart of renewal, we're one.

Tomorrow's Embrace

Stars above whisper, dreams ignite,
Calm the fears that haunt the night.
Tomorrow's promise, bright and near,
In every heartbeat, hold it dear.

The dawn unfolds, new paths await,
Hope awakens, we celebrate.
With every breath, we carve our road,
In tomorrow's arms, we'll share the load.

Clouds may gather, storms may rage,
But in our hearts, we turn the page.
Light will pierce the darkest gloom,
In tomorrow's embrace, we find room.

So step with faith, let worries cease,
In each sunrise, discover peace.
Tomorrow whispers, bold and clear,
In every moment, love draws near.

From Ruins to Radiance

In the rubble, hope takes flight,
From shattered dreams, the heart ignites.
The past may crumble, yet we arise,
Building bridges beneath the skies.

With every echo of despair,
We find the strength to rise and dare.
In cracks of stones, the flowers bloom,
From ruins lost, we chase the loom.

Light breaks through, a beacon bright,
Guiding souls through darkest night.
From ruins to radiance, we tread,
With love as compass, we are led.

So let the ashes tell our tale,
Of battles fought and spirits frail.
In every heart, a spark remains,
From ruins' grace, true strength obtains.

The Seedling's Journey

In the cradle of earth, a seed is sown,
Nurtured by rain, in silence it's grown.
Reaching for sunlight, it stretches and bends,
With dreams of the sky, its journey begins.

Through struggles and storms, it learns to survive,
With hope in its heart, it starts to thrive.
Each leaf that unfurls tells a tale of its fight,
A testament strong, a symbol of light.

Roots dig down deep, anchoring its place,
In a world full of trials, it finds its grace.
Slowly it blossoms, a miracle rare,
A seedling's journey, a story laid bare.

Through seasons of change, it stands tall and proud,
A beauty awakened, come join the crowd.
From a tiny seed sprung, a life so divine,
The seedling's journey, forever it shines.

Unwritten Pages

A blank page awaits, whispers of dreams,
Stories untold, yet bursting at seams.
With ink yet to flow, the future is wide,
Unwritten pages, let imagination glide.

In the quiet of night, ideas take flight,
Dancing like shadows, in soft, silver light.
Each line a spark, igniting the soul,
Filling the blank with stories whole.

The pen is a wand, casting spells of the mind,
Creating new worlds, leaving chaos behind.
Adventure and love, the thrill of the chase,
Unwritten pages, a magical space.

So take up the quill, let your heart guide the prose,
In the canvas of time, that only you chose.
For life is a story, waiting to be played,
Embrace every moment, on those unwritten pages.

Rebirth in Bloom

From ashes of winter, new life will arise,
With colors of spring and bright, painted skies.
Each petal that opens, a promise so bold,
Rebirth in bloom, a sight to behold.

The whispers of nature call softly and sweet,
Awakening with warmth, each garden a treat.
Life dances again in the fresh morning dew,
With scents of adventure, both old and anew.

From slumber it wakes, a glorious show,
A tapestry woven with seeds we bestow.
In the heart of the earth, the magic unfolds,
Rebirth in bloom, a story retold.

So cherish the cycles, let seasons inspire,
For hope springs eternal, like flames of a fire.
With each turn of time, let your spirit zoom,
Embrace the transformation, rebirth in bloom.

Renewal's Embrace

In the stillness of dawn, a soft light breaks,
The world gently stirs as the heart it awakes.
With whispers of change, the past fades away,
In renewal's embrace, we find our way.

Through trials and tears, we rise from the ground,
Like flowers in spring, our roots will abound.
Embracing the new, letting go of the old,
In the warmth of the sun, our stories unfold.

Each moment a gift, a chance to renew,
To write our own tale, to begin something true.
With courage as armor, we'll face what we must,
In renewal's embrace, we sow hope and trust.

So dance with the seasons, embrace all the feels,
For life is a journey, a path that reveals.
In the beauty of change, let your spirit race,
Finding strength and joy in renewal's embrace.

The Art of Reinvention

In the quiet moments of night,
We gather our dreams, taking flight.
Old skins shed, like leaves in fall,
We rise anew, we hear the call.

With every step, we learn to bend,
Rewriting stories, we start to mend.
Each failure turns to fertile ground,
In our hands, our hope is found.

We paint our lives in vibrant hues,
No path is set, no rigid views.
A canvas stretched across the skies,
With every brushstroke, our spirit flies.

Embrace the change, let fear dissolve,
In the dance of life, we evolve.
The art of reinvention, our fate,
With heart and courage, we create.

Beyond the Horizon

The sun dips low, the sky ignites,
A canvas painted with golden lights.
Waves whisper secrets of distant lands,
Calling to us with open hands.

Beyond the horizon, dreams await,
Where adventures bloom, we create.
Each step we take toward the unknown,
Unfolds a path where courage is grown.

In shadows cast by fading day,
We find the light to guide our way.
Through trials faced, we find our song,
In unity, we all belong.

Through mountain peaks and valleys deep,
We journey forth, our promise to keep.
Beyond the horizon, we shall fly,
With hearts ignited, we touch the sky.

A Path Unwritten

In the still of dawn, we stand anew,
With endless choices, skies so blue.
A blank page waits, our thoughts unfurl,
In the tapestry of life, we swirl.

Footsteps echo on the untold road,
With courage gathered, we lift the load.
A map unfolds in whispers soft,
Inviting us to dream aloft.

In moments fleeting, paths collide,
Embrace the journey, let hearts be our guide.
With hope as our lantern, we navigate,
Discovering treasures that patiently wait.

A path unwritten, a chance to be,
Each choice a brushstroke, wild and free.
In the art of living, we find our way,
With every dawn, a new chance to play.

Light After the Storm

When tempest rages and shadows fall,
We search for hope, we hear the call.
Through darkest nights and heavy rain,
A glimmer beckons, easing pain.

The clouds will part, the sun will rise,
With every dawn, the spirit flies.
Embracing strength from trials faced,
In gentle warmth, fears are erased.

Each raindrop tells a story deep,
Of battles fought, of promises to keep.
With every storm, we learn to grow,
Finding beauty in what we sow.

So let the winds of change blow strong,
For in our hearts, we all belong.
With light woven through the dark,
We rise anew, ignite the spark.

Sowing Dreams Anew

In fields of hope, we plant our dreams,
With gentle hands, we shape our schemes.
Each seed we toss, a wish takes flight,
Beneath the sun, our hearts ignite.

Through seasons' change, we'll watch them grow,
With faith in all that we don't know.
The roots entwine, the flowers bloom,
In vibrant colors, dispelling gloom.

We'll nurture each, with love and care,
Embrace the moments, bright and rare.
For in this garden, life will sing,
A chorus sweet, of everything.

So take a chance, do not delay,
Let's sow our dreams, come what may.
With every step, the path we pave,
A journey bold, the brave and brave.

Underneath Old Roots

Beneath the surface, secrets lie,
In tangled roots, where shadows sigh.
Whispers echo, stories unfold,
Of lives once lived, of treasures untold.

Through time and toil, they've grown so strong,
In ancient soil, where they belong.
The past, it clings, both firm and frail,
In every twist, a hidden tale.

With every storm, they bend, they sway,
Yet stand their ground, come what may.
In quiet strength, their wisdom flows,
A testament to all who chose.

Let's seek the roots that ground us still,
In memories' embrace, our hearts we fill.
For underneath the earth so deep,
Lie dreams of those who dared to leap.

Resilience Rekindled

In ashes cold, a spark will rise,
From shattered dreams to endless skies.
With every loss, a lesson learned,
In heart's embrace, the fire's burned.

Through trials faced, our spirits grow,
Like rivers flowing, strong and slow.
We bend but don't break, when faced with strife,
In each challenge, we find new life.

With every dawn, we stand anew,
Embracing hope, we chase what's true.
In every step, we dance with fate,
Resilience blooms, we celebrate.

So rise again, let courage guide,
Through stormy seas, we'll sail with pride.
For in our hearts, the flame won't die,
Resilience reigns, we touch the sky.

The Melody of Change

In every note, a pulse of life,
A symphony beyond all strife.
With shifting winds, the world will hum,
To rhythms new, we welcome come.

The seasons turn, the music plays,
In vibrant hues, we blend our days.
With open hearts, we move and sway,
To melodies that light the way.

Each change a chord, a sweet refrain,
In life's great dance, joy and pain.
So let us listen, to the sound,
In harmony, our dreams are found.

Together we'll weave, a tapestry,
Embracing all that's meant to be.
For in this song, our spirits soar,
The melody of change, forevermore.

Stepping into Tomorrow

With dawn's light breaking through,
Hope whispers in the breeze.
New beginnings gently bloom,
As dreams sail on the seas.

Each step a choice to make,
The path unfolds ahead.
With courage, fears we shake,
And leap where angels tread.

In shadows, sunlight glows,
Future's promise in our hands.
We dance where motion flows,
Creating vast, gentle lands.

The horizon calls us near,
With every heartbeat, rise.
Embrace the dreams we steer,
And let our spirits fly.

Pages Turned

In the book of yesterday,
Chapters filled with light and dark.
Lessons linger, come what may,
Each word leaves its vibrant mark.

New stories waiting to unfold,
Turning pages, we embrace.
Timeless tales in colors bold,
History etched in this space.

Memories with each stroke made,
Whispers of the past reside.
Yet within, we find the shade,
Of dreams that still abide.

The ink flows like a stream,
Woven tales of joy and strife.
In every heart, a gleam,
As we write the song of life.

A Symphony of First Notes

In the silence, dreams ignite,
Softly, whispers start to play.
Melodies take fragile flight,
Painting skies in shades of gray.

Strikes of keys and strings collide,
Harmonies rise, wild and free.
In this moment, worlds collide,
Music wraps around the plea.

Each note a step toward the stars,
Echoes dance with sweet delight.
Bridges built from Mars to bars,
Unfolding magic in the night.

As rhythms pulse like heartbeats,
Unfurling stories left untold.
The symphony of life repeats,
In every dream, a note of gold.

The Resilient Heart

Beneath the weight of sorrow,
Hope blooms like flowers in spring.
Every beat, a new tomorrow,
From pain, the heart takes wing.

In storms, it learns to dance,
With every crack, it finds its song.
Through trials, it takes a stance,
Growing strong where it belongs.

Though shadows fall and fade,
The heart will rise, it won't concede.
In love's light, fears cascade,
Resilience rooted like a seed.

Embraced by warmth and care,
It pulses with a steadfast grace.
A melody beyond compare,
The resilient heart holds space.

The Courage to Begin

In shadows deep, we find our spark,
A whisper soft, igniting the dark.
With trembling hands, we take the leap,
Dreams await, our hearts to keep.

The path is unclear, yet bold we stand,
With hope as our guide, we take command.
Each step we forge, a story to tell,
In courage found, we break the shell.

The echoes of doubt may fill the air,
Yet trust in ourselves, banish despair.
With every breath, our spirits rise,
In the face of fear, we claim the prize.

So here's to the dawn, the chance to start,
With passion anew, we open our heart.
For in every beginning, there lies a chance,
To dance with our dreams, and boldly advance.

New Threads to Weave

In the loom of life, threads intertwine,
Colors of joy, and shades that align.
We gather our stories, both old and new,
Crafting a tapestry, vibrant and true.

Each strand like a memory, woven with care,
In patterns of laughter, love, and despair.
With gentle hands, we create our space,
A fabric of moments, time can't erase.

Though some threads may fray, and others may fade,
The beauty remains in the choices we made.
So here's to the craft, the life that we weave,
In every connection, we learn to believe.

With every new stitch, a story unfolds,
In colors of courage, the future beholds.
Together, we stand, united and free,
Weaving our lives into history's tapestry.

Embrace the Unfamiliar

In the shadow of comfort, new horizons call,
With hearts wide open, we'll risk it all.
The unknown awaits, a canvas so vast,
In letting go gently, we release the past.

With every brave step into the unknown,
We find hidden treasures, in winds overblown.
The world is a puzzle, each piece to unveil,
In learning to dance, we shall not fail.

Embrace the strange, let curiosity lead,
For in every encounter, our spirits succeed.
With laughter and wonder, we'll break down the walls,
In the warmth of connection, true freedom calls.

So rise with the sun, let your heart take flight,
In the beauty of change, in the still of night.
For life is a journey, rich and profound,
In the unfamiliar, our joy will be found.

The First Breath of a New Day

As dawn breaks gently, the world comes alive,
In hues of amber, the dreams start to thrive.
With the first breath taken, we shake off the night,
A canvas awaits, it's time to ignite.

The morning whispers secrets, fresh and anew,
In every soft moment, sky painted blue.
With open hearts, we step into grace,
Each second a promise, a new embrace.

Chasing away shadows, the sun fills the air,
With hope as our compass, we rise without fear.
Let laughter be sung, let kindness prevail,
In the warmth of the sun, our spirits set sail.

So take in the beauty, each moment a gift,
With gratitude deep, let your heart gently lift.
For in every new day, possibilities sway,
Embracing the dawn, we journey away.